EASY READING INFORMATION SERIES

SUGAR

Written by O. B. Gregory
Illustrated by Elsie Wrigley

Library of Congress Cataloging in Publication Data

Gregory, O. B. (Olive Barnes), 1940-
Sugar.

(Easy reading information series)
Summary: Explains briefly and simply how we get sugar from sugar cane and sugar beets. Includes questions and a vocabulary list.
1. Sugar—Juvenile literature. [1. Sugar]
I. Wrigley, Elsie, ill. II. Title. III. Series.
TP378.2.G73 664'.12 81-11920
ISBN 0-86625-169-3 AACR2

ROURKE PUBLICATIONS, INC.
Windermere, Fla. 32786

SUGAR

Do you like sweets and chocolate?

Do you like cakes and puddings?

I bet you do.

All these things are sweet.

They are sweet because
they contain sugar.

This is the story of how
we get our sugar.

Many plants contain sugar.

Most of our sugar comes from
the stem of the sugar cane.

Sugar cane is really a tall grass
with a thick stem.

The stem is about two inches thick.

The sugar is inside the stem.

Look at the picture.

You can see the thick stem
and the long leaves.

Some of our sugar comes from
the West Indies.

The West Indies are islands
many miles away.

In the West Indies it is always hot
and there is plenty of rain.

Sugar cane plants need a hot climate.

They also need plenty of rain.

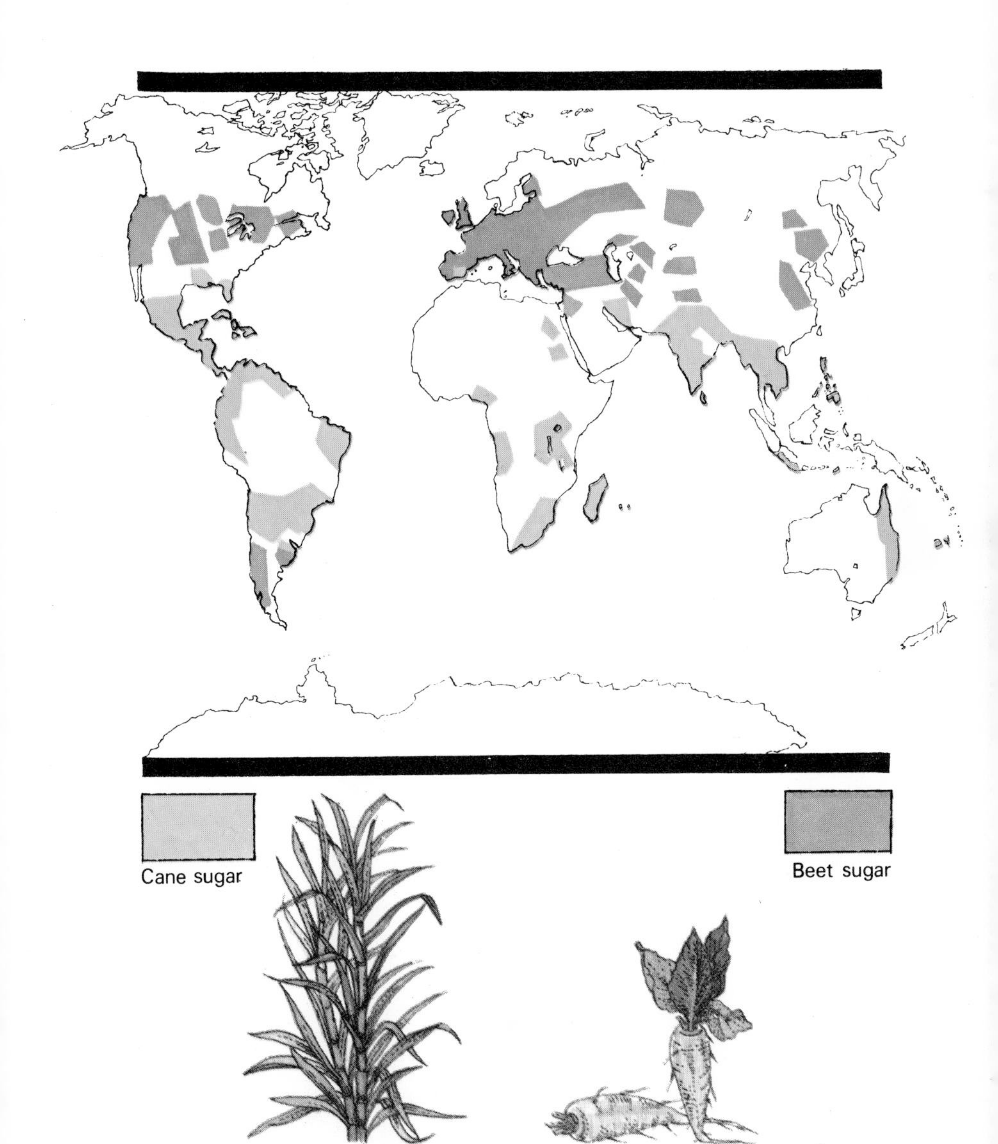
Cane sugar
Beet sugar

This is how a new sugar cane plant
is grown.

First of all, a short piece of cane
is cut from an old plant.

The short piece of cane
is then put in the ground.

The piece of cane grows quickly
in the wet ground.

About one year later the cane is ripe.

It is about twelve feet tall
and is ready for cutting.

Sometimes the work is done
by machine.

Sometimes the work is done by hand.

The men who cut the cane
use sharp knives.

They cut through the bottom
of the cane, close to the ground.

Then they cut off the leaves.

The cane is taken to the factory.

At the factory
the cane is cut into smaller pieces.

Then it has to be crushed.

It is crushed between big rollers.

The rollers crush the cane
and this gets the juice out.

The juice is inside the stem
of the sugar cane.

When the rollers have crushed the cane
the juice goes into big tanks.

The sugar is in the juice.

The juice is brown at first.

It is boiled.

After a time, the juice gets thicker.

Lumps of raw sugar
begin to form.

The mixture is spun around
in big drums.

The thick juice is run off.

The raw sugar is left
in the drum.

The raw sugar is then put
on board ship.

The sugar is not put into sacks.

It is taken to the ship
and put straight in the hold.

When the ship gets to its destination
the sugar is taken out.

It is then washed and boiled.

This takes away the brown color
and clean, white sugar is left.

Not all sugar
comes from sugar cane.

Some of it comes from sugar beet.

It has a fat, white root
which contains the sugar.

The seeds are sown in spring.

By autumn the roots are ready
to be pulled up.

The leaves are cut off
and given to cows or sheep to eat.

Sometimes the roots
are pulled up by hand.

Sometimes the work is done
by machine.

The beets are then
taken to the factory.

First of all, they are washed.

Then they are cut into small pieces.

The pieces are put into tanks of water.

The sugar comes out of the beets
and into the water.

The water is then boiled
and sugar is left behind.

THINGS TO WRITE

1. What plant does sugar come from? (4)
2. How thick is the sugar cane stem? (4)
3. Where does our sugar come from? (6)
4. Do sugar cane plants need a hot climate? (6)
5. Do sugar cane plants need plenty of rain? (6)
6. When is the cane ready for cutting? (10)
7. How is the cutting done? (10)
8. Where do the men cut the cane? (10)
9. Where is the cane taken? (10)

10. How is the can crushed? (12)

11. Why is the cane crushed? (12)

12. What color is the juice at first? (14)

13. What is done to the mixture? (14)

14. What is left in the drum? (14)

15. How is raw sugar transported? (16)

16. What is done to take away the brown color? (16)

17. Does all sugar come from sugar cane? (18)

18. How else do we get sugar? (18)

19. What does a sugar beet look like? (18)

20. Which part of the beet contains the sugar? (18)

VOCABULARY

SUGAR CANE — a tropical plant from which sugar is made. It is a tall grass.

SUGAR BEET — a tropical plant with a white root from which sugar is made.

CHOCOLATE — a dark brown, sweet substance. It is used in ice cream, candy and cakes.

STEM — the stalk of a plant. It grows above the ground.

MACHINE — a device consisting of several different parts which work together to perform a single function.

FACTORY — a building where many people work to produce a certain type of goods.

JUICE — the liquid which is pressed from a plant.

DRUMS — large pots which hold liquids.

ROOT — the part of the plant which grows underground.

CLIMATE — the general weather of a certain region. This includes air temperature, air pressure and sunshine.